**How to run a technology company**

**by Adrian Corbuleanu**

**September 2018**

## Contents

Specialize ............................................................................................................................. 3
Recruit right ........................................................................................................................ 6
Stay customer centered ...................................................................................................... 8
Build your business on fundamentals ................................................................................ 10
Deliver business value ....................................................................................................... 12
Operate agile ..................................................................................................................... 14
Quality and reliability ........................................................................................................ 16
Make strategic decisions ................................................................................................... 19
Stay away from long sales cycles ...................................................................................... 21
Business network .............................................................................................................. 22

## Specialize

Technology is, by definition, a business of expertise. If you talk to people or read online content, you will see that a lot of experts will advise you to pick a niche and dig deep inside it. A niche is usually defined as a confined set of technologies + an industry such as building ".NET Solutions for Education" or "wooCommerce Solutions for the Golf Apparel Industry" or "iOS Solutions for Plastic Surgeons".

Specializing and working in a niche has clear advantages: in time you will get to "own" the technology really well, product/platform management wise you will make a serious business impact, it will also be easier for you to get to the market, advertising will be less costly, business networking will be more impactful etc. Some people will advise you to pick your niche even narrower such as ".NET Solutions for Florida based Charter Schools" or "Mobile CRM Solutions for California based Boat Brokerage Companies" (in my opinion that is actually debate-able if it makes sense to do).

Specialization usually means:

- displaying your and/or your staff education in the niche

- displaying your and/or your staff professional experience in the niche (you can start with a handful of smaller projects, just make sure they are targeted)

- gathering a significant number of customers testimonials and references

But stronger ways to show specialization are:

- speaking at industry events

- getting to be featured in local or national media

- having an Advanced Degree in your niche (e.g. "XYZ Developer has a PhD in Statistics or Big Data")

- displaying an outstanding achievement (e.g. "XYZ Company released an Android app that got 250,000 downloads in the Play Store").

Specialization builds trust and trust is what closes new business.

My experience with getting specialized in a certain technology and/or industry: it is always a good idea to kind of try and "time" your specialization. Timing is a big deal in the survival equation of a new business so having that vision is very important. Remember: timing, team, market, problem solved, product/platform and only after that funding.

You want to specialize in established technologies and growing industries. For example technologies wise: .NET is current and established, iOS and Android are current, LAMP is current, Word Press is current, wooCommerce is current etc. Industries wise: healthcare is growing, tourism and hospitality is growing, online marketing services are growing, e-commerce is growing, gaming industry is growing, IoT is growing etc.

Myth: "You need to specialize in things that are cool and everybody talks about them online, on TV, on Facebook, at Trade Shows and Conferences!"

No, you don't. As a matter of fact I'd be cautious. Especially with concepts like block chain, AI/Big Data, distributed systems, smart contracts etc. Or with some sexy looking technology, e.g. React, Vue etc. React currently has 2% of the market, it did not grow significantly as a technology over the last 12-24 month and there are no business related reasons to believe things will dramatically change in the near future.

If you have a call / career interest / very serious reason to specialize in a certain technology, by all means do it. But don't do it just because you hear some buzz words at a Conference or because your best friend says it's cool.

The same thing goes about industries, try & "feel" the industry / industries that you pick: they need to be a fit with your structure and beliefs as well. Some growing industries will not be your cup of tea, e.g. we constantly get requests to build solutions for the cannabis industry and we constantly turn them down as we do not want to be associated with that industry. Just the fact that medicinal cannabis is a current and growing industry does not mean that you have to work in it.

Technologies wise we also usually recommend specializing in established technologies rather than super new / unknown ones. These would be technologies that were around for at least a decade (two decades better). The reason is that a lot of the new technologies are unstable and would potentially have a negative impact on the quality of your product / service: that will be perceived as your company's inability to deliver a quality product. The open source community is getting better and better and open source code is clearly of better quality than what we had 15-20 years ago, still it is a good idea to specialize in well supported technologies.

When you will become the go-to person for a certain technology and/or industry in your community, you will see that you will start getting a lot of complimentary and unsolicited inbound leads. These will be based on the respect you were able to convey as an expert in your field.

One last word here: specialization takes time. Be patient and stay at it. Specialization is not something you achieve in 3-6 month. It takes years of work, pursued opportunities, lessons learned and self-education.

## Recruit right

Recruiting right is paramount for any technology business. And recruiting right is hard.

From developers to sales and account management personnel, from project managers to graphic designers the quality of your company will be impacted by the quality of the people you will attract and retain.

While I am not an HR expert, I advise for recruiting a Core Team (some companies call it a Senior Leadership Team) who walked the walk and empower them to recruit their teams. You want to run a flat Organization as well with max. 3 layers.

Advertise extensively, interview thoroughly and do not recruit in a rush. "We hire fast and we fire fast" is never a good idea.

I had a good experience using my own network of former co-workers, LinkedIn, Indeed.com and even staff recruiters. A lot of the sales people popped up by themselves during trade shows or they were hard and consistent at work trying to sell me services, so I did not really have to spend a lot of money on recruiting activities. LinkedIn in particular is fantastic in locating professionals. For contractors Upwork.com is a great site with virtually unlimited resources, however you have to check reviews, interview and test thoroughly.

When working with remote teams always check the staff's location. We had instances where people miss represented their location (e.g. advertising they were located in Seattle and they were in fact located in … Africa!). It is relatively easy to check somebody's physical location with his driver's license and his/her latest utility bill.

Always hire based on character first, then skills. Skills can be added, people can get trained. Character cannot be changed. Here, I am going to say this one more time: do not overlook this and do not cut corners: it is a very important aspect!

Pay attention to the culture you want to instill. You and your small team of managers will drive the company's culture. If you are an uptight person, you will have an uptight company but then you have to make sure you recruit accordingly. If you like open office spaces and want to ride scooters while at work, then make it like and make sure you recruit people who like that. Companies don't realize but when it comes to recruiting employees, culture is as important as the salary you offer and sometimes even more important. Culture is also extremely important when it comes to retaining employees long term: if they feel good with the company and they make good money, people will not easily leave your company.

A little more on company's culture as it is extremely important. You want to promote a culture of performance, self-accountability, collaboration and peers respect. You also want to recruit *nice people*. It is a myth that at work you do not make friends. It is also a myth that at work you somehow have to be dry/mean/short in order to accomplish performance.

Culture is:

- creating a work environment where people brainstorm on challenging projects

- creating a work environment where people are appreciated and celebrated

- discouraging low level practices (back stabbing, "cover your butt" kind of thing, "point fingers" etc.

Culture is not:

- installing ping pong tables

- having wild happy hours

- sipping coffee and eating donuts while clapping in Friday morning "employees appreciation meetings" (also ridiculously called "shout out" meetings)

When it comes to recruiting for your technical team you need to learn how to advertise, interview and test to attract the high performers. A lot of developers "look good" at a glance but there are actually big differences between average/just okay developers and high performers.

I have separate blogs and speeches on this topic but here let's just say that a great developer, as opposed to an average developer, has the following extra treats: a) creativity b) agility c) specialization d) outstanding achievements (e.g. Certifications, Advanced Degrees, Patents or Inventions) e) many and great references.

And never forget: as soon as you start building up your team, they will have a strong opinion on who to hire. Why? It is very simple: human nature. People want to work with people who are like them.

## Stay customer centered

Customer support and customer service in general had been going down in quality for two decades+. Starting with the offshore-ing and outsourcing movement of the '90s and picking up after the burst of the dot com bubble, we got to a point where it was really challenging to get good old professional prompt over the phone support.

Back in the days I managed the Tech Support Group of a Minneapolis, MN company that had just been re-capitalized and was operating in a start-up mode. The company was an Internet Devices Manufacturer. We designed L4-L7 Internet traffic aggregators and WAN redundancy devices (basically intelligent routers). The company was smart, small and very challenged by its much bigger and stronger competition: companies like Cisco, F5, Radware.

While I was delivering quite a bit of hands-on programming and tech support myself, like in any small company I had to wear other hats as well. One of the was Tech Support Manager. We would literally hold our customers hands and would not go home until our device was totally deployed and working as expected in their networks. In time the CEO of our company got a lot of feed-back from directs customers, resellers and other business partners who congratulated him for the "world class support" (that's what they called it, not me) his business was delivering. While the devices themselves had certain flaws and they were not suitable for some of the applications, many customers said that it was our tech and customer support that kept the company in business during very difficult years (2001- 2006) for the IT industry. Today that company deployed more than 10,000 devices, it is very profitable and growing.

Depending on the complexity of your business and on the service / product you deliver you may need to deliver more or less direct customer support. But the idea is the same: remain super focused on your customers needs and genuinely help them out to succeed. When your customers are successful, you are successful.

In a world of chat bots, AI that does not really work in the customers interest (or does not work at all to sustain a decent conversation for that matter) and outsourced support groups placed in exotic geographies, be your client's support champion! Believe in it and execute it every day!

Staying customer centered means understanding and appreciating your customers business and being able to align and implement the technology you deliver with his/her business objectives. I.e. "We are a mid size e-commerce platform that sells auto parts and we need to implement zero downtime deployments of cross selling and upselling features." => you need to flawlessly support that. It also means truly supporting your customer and his staff not only technically flawless but also in accordance to their business needs, hours of operations, terms of communication etc.

Staying customer centered does not necessarily mean boasting it big on your website "We love our customers!". Talk is cheap. Back it up with action. Customer appreciation events, small gifts, freebies sent over are fine but, again, you will need much more substance than just those.

From a bigger picture business standpoint, when you are customer centered you obviously:

- reduce the rate of returns

- increase the rate of new business referrals

- increase the rate of repeat business (crucial for any business)

- help out sales and pre-sales (based on your established reputation)

- you save yourself a lot of money and headaches

At the end of this section, I will circle back on staff. I believe it is important because a lot of companies make the following mistake: they assign second rated staff. "Okay, you are not the smartest bulb in this room. We are going to put you in Customer Support." Do not make that mistake: assign some of your best staff in Support. They will face customers on a daily basis and they will build the image of your company. Assign some of your best trained and best soft skills staff to face your customers. That applies to both After Sales Support and Pre Sales Support.

## Build your business on fundamentals

Have you seen some of these newer trends? "We sign in users. A lot of them. Millions of them. and that's ALL what we care about! We don't need to make a profit right away. That can come later after we grow our userbase. Let's sign in a lot of free users!"

With all due respect for companies like Uber, Instacart (and even Facebook back in their days) for most of the other companies, this model will not be sustainable. The reason is that, relatively fast, you have to get to a point to build not only critical mass (which is very difficult in itself) but in fact a *tremendous* number of users. To be able to afford to loose money for years (like Uber) you need tens and hundreds of millions in investments which is really a fantasy to think you can actually secure. Then you have to have a very well thought strategy to convert those users into high paying users without loosing them (not possible in many scenarios).

Instead start lean, solid and build your business on economical fundamentals. Release working product / platform fast and start signing in users. Break even as soon as you can. If you can break even by the end of the first year, that's great! If not, make it your objective to break even and to start making money in max. 18 to 24 month. If you can be profitable in less than 6 month, that's even better! (WWS was a profitable tech company as soon as it's first year as it did not raise funds from investors and they started to secure projects in less than 3 month after start).

Building your business on economic fundamentals means:

- Minimize expenses

- Maximize profits

- Check your balances *every month* rather than every quarter or every year

- Work agile (we have a separate section on this)

- Hold yourself as a CEO accountable

- Build repeat revenue models rather than constant new users acquisition models

- Establish a great reputation in your industry / community

- Avoid different business "schematics" and practices (if it sounds speculative, stay away from it)

- Stay away from derivatives, short sells and other things like that

And remember: if you are in business to make money and everybody expects that. Including IRS. So make sure you report accurately and correctly to taxes every year. Do not skip tax returns.

## Deliver business value

Delivering business value is paramount when running a tech business. A lot of tech start-ups get out of business because they do tech for the sake for tech. Not keeping in mind your clients business goals is a common mistake that has to be avoided by all means. Designing average tech, commodities tech or, even worse, buggy tech will not cut it either.

You deliver business value when you design a well thought e-commerce front end that increases conversions.

You deliver business value when you implement an automatic, continuous builds and delivery process that reduces time spent with manual deployments with 70% and it minimizes the system downtime.

You deliver business value when you design your e-commerce solution with SEO in mind (i.e. on-page SEO). This will drive inbound search engine traffic and it will increase sales for your customer.

You deliver business value when you involve a very sophisticated AI developer from your team. This developer implements and supports a smooth business attire dressing recommendations solution based on users input in online filled out questionnaire.

As you can see from these examples delivering business value is not just saving in software production costs. It is that as well, but it is equally important to be able to contribute to your client's bottom line by increasing your client's revenue.

The value that you deliver has to be measurable. In $$$ amounts saved upfront, in time saved due to improved processes and in $$$ generated on the output side. Prove yourself. Implement a system to be able to measure that value and constantly communicate it with your customers.

Business value is:

- implementing high quality, high business impact products and platforms

- implementing platforms that scale up

- implementing platforms that are low in maintenance costs and upgrades

- both saving money with production costs and increasing revenues for your customer

Business value is not:

- implementing average quality or high maintenance solutions

- just saving some money upfront (for example by off-shore-ing development)

## Operate agile

At WWS we are big fans of agility. We believe it is nowadays essential for start-ups survival to operate in an agile way. Start-ups should act in an agile way both in pre-revenue mode and in after revenue mode. In fact, they should plan on operating agile for a long time. Think pass series A, B or C or even if they make it to go public.

It is always very healthy for a company to operate agile.

We preach agility on both the technical/product implementation & processes side and or the actual business side. We like the lean start-up model that some companies adopt today with low overhead and the ability to pivot fast if need be.

Iterating and doing things in small fast steps with immediate customer feed-back will help you stay out of trouble. Technically, writing code that allows for late requirements changes and eliminating inconsistencies early in the process will save you a lot of money and headaches.

As you can see from the Agile Manifesto, building agile software has some very special treats. Per the Manifesto agility has the main goal of delivering "working software", it emphasizes on "customer collaboration over contracts negotiation" and "welcomes change" no matter how late in the development process.

From a business standpoint, running a lean business is even more impactful. Controlling costs with staff is key as staff is by far the highest expense of a tech business. You want to be able to scale up and down in agile way but you have to be able to do it without impacting morale. We do recommend having a core team that is invested in the business (hence paid part equity / stock) while maintaining a team of on-demand high quality contractors who can work on specific assignments. This structure will particularly help you out prior to your take off when cash is scarce and you have to make it to securing and collecting on your next paid opportunity.

Agility has some pitfalls. One of them is that, in order to work well, pretty much everybody has to be agile: engineering team, product owner, management, client. Many times, the client is not agile and you will not get your desired feed-back even if you did everything very agile. You need to walk in your clients shoes, understand what motivates the client and incentivize your client to move in an agile way. As a smaller company you will have less issues with management of your own company.

Agility is about skills, but it is also a lot about *mentalities*. Here we can circle back to recruiting the right staff for your business, it is extremely important for you to recruit agile staff and generally staff that has not only technical skills and experience but also a great attitude towards working in agile teams. Staff who points fingers, back stabs, steps on the break, is negligent with their work has nothing to do with agility and should not have any place in your Organization. Being able to build a culture where everybody feels like they are moving towards the same goal (it's *very* personal) is as important as difficult it is to do.

Agility is:

- your company's ability to move ahead lean, fast and efficient

- your company's ability to pivot without incurring major costs

- your product/platforms team ability to work in an agile way

- your ability is a company to engage customers to be agile inside your process as well

Agility is not:

- cutting corners in development or doing a sloppy job

- calling yourself a SCRUM Master but doing a slower job and an Enterprise Waterfall PM

Agility will keep you safe from:

- making expensive Platform/Product Management mistakes

- spending a lot of cash on staff and/or Products/Platforms before you become profitable

- releasing software with minimal or no customer business impact

- swings / trends in the market

## Quality and reliability

There are many companies out there who talk about the quality of their products and some of them can substantiate it. Over the last two decades the web development tools improved, the web hosting improved as well, the bandwidth grew up and the technologists became more experienced and more creative.

Still, in many areas, the quality of web assets still suffers. You still run into a lot of poorly designed sites. You still need to go get a cup of coffee to load up some pretty basic pages on your laptop. Not all the sites out there are responsive and quite a few are straight outdated (they look like they technology of the '90s!). Security wise a lot of sites are timing bombs exposing their owners to liability and tarnishing their reputation in business.

There is actually still a huge gap between the newer, sexier, minimalistic sites and the old feel dusty / outdated / slow-like-Christmas / poorly structured websites.

The spread of mobile devices complicated things even more. 10 years after the start of mass adoption in mobile technologies there are still many late adopters and still a lot of work to do to improve the mobile experience of the customers.

Be a champion of quality. Do not just verbally express your company's priority in developing quality product but live it & breadth it. Show it in what you do every day. Believing and executing with quality is actually hard because it's a lot of work and sacrifice and it involves culture and beliefs.

Think Mercedes all the time. Or Lexus. Or Lincoln. Or Caddy. Nothing under those brands. Imagine yourself driving your car to work and forgetting your coffee without a lid in your car's cupholder. You need to be able to do 80 on the highway without spilling a drop of coffee. Your car / software platform needs to "glue itself" to the road and to smoothly "purr" like a cat when you wildly step down on your accelerator.

Test, test, test. Obviously to achieve quality you have to test quite a bit and to improve yourself in iterations quite a bit. Do it. Do not cut corners. Stay at it in a diligent way. There is no other option.

Some people make the mistake to think that working agile means giving up on quality. Not at all. Agility does not mean "messy code" or "crappy solutions". Agility means quality code in fast iterations. (Agility does not mean "no documentation" either but that's a different discussion).

During my Corporate tenures I had many discussions on quality at different levels of different Organizations. I always got great feed-back as I was always a quality freak! ☺ Actually I should not say a freak! I was always somebody passionate about quality and that was not really only at work, it was also somehow a part of my every day private life as well, i.e. I always liked a good quality car, a good quality house or apartment, a good quality vacation, a good quality food. I guess it was in my DNA. It is great to have quality in your DNA!

Think Apple. Who does not like the UI/UX of Apple, a trillion $$$$$ company now? But, if you think about it, it's not just the UI. Their OS had always had few flaws: it was always stable and rarely crashed (as opposed to my PC or even my old Unix station that somehow managed to crash every week). Their platforms are fast and smooth (as opposed to a lot of the PCs which struggle with speed even at low levels of software loads). Apple also gets less viruses. At some point in time they had virtually zero viruses on their devices. The iPhone, in particular, is a great physical product as well, made out of high end materials and mechanically designed like a piece of jewelry. Some of the other hardware components, i.e. the embedded camera are also world class in their categories. With their latest model X, Apple is also on the forefront of consumer facing image recognition technologies which work very well.

Write software like Apple. You will be more than ok.

In terms of reliability, that is a very important aspect of your business success as well. Your clients need to be able to rely on you as a company. In good and bad times, they need to know you are there for them.

Too many companies nowadays come and go. They are in to make a quick buck. If they pick up traction they sell, M&A or simply just quit and go to the beach. Some of them go public as they believe in their mission but a lot of them do not (we actually have a few samples here in town of start-ups CEOs who did not think for a second to serve their community or to build any kind of legacy).

Do not be one of those. Believe in your mission. Be resourceful and reliable for your customers. Be there for your customers.

You started a tech company to improve the lunch experience of public school children while reducing costs? Great! Then execute on that mission. Be the greatest technology resource for the children, for the school's admin staff and for educators! And do it consistently. And do it for a long time. If you get to the point to pick up traction, grow organically and stick around. Get more schools under your umbrella and create more jobs in your community. Expand State wide and even regionally and keep the same level of fantastic support for your students and parents. Do not sell anytime soon and do not start cutting corners.

Yes, you should definitely have profit goals and economical performance KPIs that you should meet but hopefully that will not mean artificially imposing thresholds based on 3$^{rd}$ party criteria or doing things that would not align with your mission and with the children and parents interest.

## Make strategic decisions

Sometimes you have to make strategic decisions. Now, I cannot just go ahead and tell you guys: "Go ahead and make some strategic decisions!" or "Make sure you make at least one strategic decision a month!" because that's not how it works. You have to essentially be able to spot the opportunities when they arise and pull the trigger.

If you read in the tech literature you will see that most of the icon CEOs that you heard of (including Steve Jobs, Bill Gates, Elon Musk) made a series of tough / strategic decisions to grow their businesses.

Steve Jobs gave $1 Bil. (!) credit to AT&T when he had a hard time convincing them to position the relatively new (an unknown) iPhone. That's $1 Bil. with a B. The Board of Apple thought Steve was nuts! He also decided to only open up high end retail stores in location with nice / expensive real estate. His focus on in-store (and out of the store) free education on Apple's products was instrumental in the iPhone's take off.

Bill Gates decided to build not only a new attractive and easy to use OS for the PC but also business applications like Office and developers tools like MS Visual Suite during a period of time when these kinds of applications were only for specialists and usually very expensive. You can say that Bill was one of the pioneers in the "democratization" of Information Technology.

Elon invested in his last penny in Tesla and Space-X. He was walking around joking that he had to borrow money for ... rent! He invested over 100 Mil. $$$$$ that he cleared from his PayPal sale. During the Great Recession of 2008-2012 the investors needed re-assurance that Elon is serious about his new electrical car concept and he reassured them! Some people don't remember but at that time the economy was so bad, even GM almost got out of business (in fact GM needed a Government bail-out, which Elon did not).

You will have to make all kinds of strategic decisions when:

- pick up your product, platform and technology
- pick up your team(s)
- pivot
- offer business terms
- build reputation

- establish alliances
- expand / contract / take side steps

Do not be afraid to make strategic decisions. Use consultants if you need them but "feel it in your stomach" when you do it and assume responsibility!

## Stay away from long sales cycles

Since day #1 in our business we stayed away from long sales cycles. Long sales cycles drain your energy and resources and distract you from generating new business or from focusing on organically growing the business you already have.

It is our experience (and many others from our network) that the best business you can get happens relatively fast and without huge "push-ups" so to speak. Of course, this will depend on the industry you are in and the size of your clients and many other factors but as a general rule of thumb "good business closes fast" or never closes.

What is fast? You will ask.

Well, it's almost never 6 month or a year!

Some people will pop numbers out of their hat and they will tell you that it should take between (and here you will hear different numbers depending on who you are talking to) let's 12 and 15 interactions with somebody before you close a deal. Some others will back it up with data, but the idea remains the same.

Some of my best deals closed in 3(!) business days after the initial meet & greet with the client. Some others took 2 weeks. Some others up to 1 month. But that's it! That's about it! I close 90% of my business in 4 to 7 interactions with the prospect. And I rarely sweat it.

Unless we have an on-going business relationship with an entity, we have a 60 business days cut off on all the projects we bid on.

Sales are numbers games. For every 100 prospects you talk to you end up with 2 to 5 "warm" leads. Play that conservative and say 2, not 3, 4 or 5. For every 10 warm leads only 1 generally closes. So the real percentage is .2%. That's 2 in 1,000! Play the game accordingly, target right and increase the numbers of 1000s of people you get in front of, diligently follow up with them for up to 60 days after the initial contact and do not worry about anything else.

## Business network

I left business networking at the end but that does not mean it's less important as a topic.

In fact business networking and building alliances with trusted business partners are a great thing to do! People underestimate the importance of business networking or they do it wrong.

Business networking mean building long term solid mutually beneficial relationships / alliances / collaborations with other companies / services providers who are not in a direct competition with your business, in fact they somehow target the same market with you but in an adjacent line of business.

If you are a software development company, build relationships with online marketing companies.

If you are a video production company, build business relationships with online retailers or e-commerce companies.

If you sell business clothing for millennials online, build a relationship with a shoes company for millennials.

If you are a talented graphic designer build a relationship with a web or mobile development company.

You get the idea.

Always work selfless and refer business out first. Continue to refer business to your partners. Do not worry what you are getting back. Keep referring. They will definitely refer you back as soon as they can. Most of the people are nice and it is human nature to return a service to somebody.

Business networking means:

- actively working on building meaningful long term business relationships with the people you meet

- creating business situations where $1 + 1 = 3$ (it is not that obvious how to do that but if you think about it, you can do it)

- delivering value to your new business partners before you expect them to deliver any value to you (we used to refer 3 leads out for each lead we got in for the first 12 month of a new partnership or alliance)

Business networking does not mean:

- attending conferences and shows, handing out business cards then forgetting about it

- attending conferences and shows, grabbing other people business cards then forgetting about them

- attending tech events but playing shy and putting yourself in the corner of the room

- attending events, jumping on people and immediately trying to sell them some of your services

- (not even) passively following up with e-mails or phone calls 2-3 weeks after an event

Also, be there for your network. I got countless business referrals and opportunities in my local community by just showing up consistently to events and meetups. With this particular event in town I used to joke that I should be recruited as an Organizer as I was there for two years on a weekly basis every Wed with very few interruptions (mainly only during the Winter Holidays and one week during the summer). While other companies were present very inconsistently and most of the companies will show up their faces once or twice, then forever vanished!

Organizing your own event is always a good idea. If you get to run such an initiative plan it long term and target your audience and speakers right. The best thing is to have one of your staff members (usually a Marketing Manager or Director of Marketing) in charge with the meetup as part of his/her weekly job responsibilities.

I have separate blogs on how to business network effectively in Miami and what are the best events to attend (there are a lot of meetups in Miami every week and year around but there are in fact a handful of them who will be worth your time)

As a rule of thumb, the bigger the event (i.e. over 200 participants), the better. But there are some smaller events that will be good quality as well. You just have to do a little leg work and figure them out (or ask us!).

In Miami events like e-Merge, SUP-X and IT Palooza will always be great opportunities for networking while other 2<sup>nd</sup> tier events like Refresh will also deliver a solid stream of new business networking opportunities.

Nationally you should attend events like Synapse, DISRUPT, South By South West, Mobile Word Congress, Geekwire Summit, Microsoft Ignite, Crowdsourcing Week etc.

Do not waste time with really small events (20, 30 or even people) even if they are free. Our experience shows they will not deliver the right networking opportunities for you.

www.ingramcontent.com/pod-product-compliance
Lightning Source LLC
Chambersburg PA
CBHW031522210526
45464CB00007B/3004